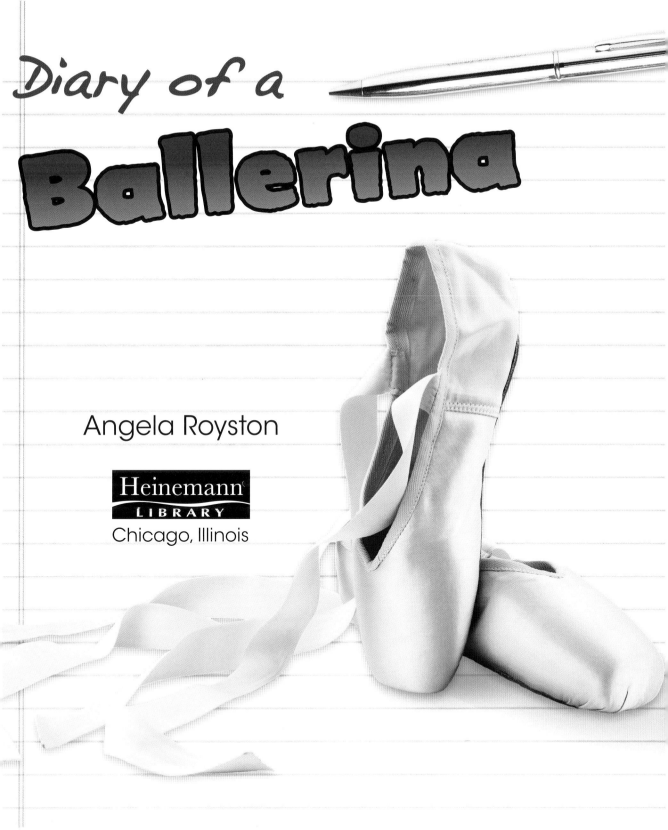

Diary of a Ballerina

Angela Royston

Heinemann
LIBRARY
Chicago, Illinois

Edited by Daniel Nunn, Rebecca Rissman, and Catherine Veitch
Designed by Cynthia Akiyoshi
Picture research by Ruth Blair
Production by Victoria Fitzgerald
Originated by Capstone Global Library Ltd
Printed in the United States of America in
North Mankato, Minnesota

122013
007920RP

Library of Congress Cataloging-in-Publication Data
Royston, Angela, 1945-
  Ballerina / Angela Royston.
    p. cm.—(Diary of a. . .)
  Includes bibliographical references and index.
  ISBN 978-1-4329-7579-1 (hb)—ISBN 978-1-4329-7586-9 (pb)
1. Ballerinas—Juvenile literature. I. Title.
GV1787.5.R687 2013
  792.8—dc23   2012046856

Acknowledgments
We would like to thank the following for permission to reproduce
photographs: Corbis pp. 8 (© Yuan Xue Jun/Redlink), 17 (©
Robbie Jack), 20 (© Nathalie Darbellay/Sygma), 22 (© Yang
Liu), 23 (© Bettmann); Getty Images pp. 5 (Washington Post),
7 (Hybrid Images), 9 (Maria Teijeiro), 11 (BENHAMOU/DUFOUR/
Gamma-Rapho), 14 (David Fischer), 16 (DIETER NAGL/AFP),
18 (Sven Creutzmann/Mambo Photo/), 26 (Wendy Maeda/The
Boston Globe), 27 (KIMMO MANTYLA/AFP); Shutterstock pp. title
page (© Yuganov Konstantin), contents page, 21 (© Yuri Arcurs),
4, 25 (© Igor Bulgarin), 6 (© Felix Mizioznikov), 10 (© Cyhel),
13 (© Olesia Bilkei), 19 (© testing), 28 (© eans), 30 (© Brent
Hofacker); Superstock pp. 12 (Ingram Publishing), 15 (Image
Source), 24 (Stock Connection).

Background and design features reproduced with permission of
Shutterstock. Cover photograph of ballerina stretching at barre
reproduced with permission of Corbis (© Image Source).

We would like to thank Annie Besarra for her invaluable help in
the preparation of this book.

Every effort has been made to contact copyright holders of
material reproduced in this book. Any omissions will be rectified
in subsequent printings if notice is given to the publisher.

All the Internet addresses (URLs) given in this book were valid at
the time of going to press. However, due to the dynamic nature
of the Internet, some addresses may have changed, or sites may
have changed or ceased to exist since publication. While the
author and publisher regret any inconvenience this may cause
readers, no responsibility for any such changes can be accepted
by either the author or the publisher.

Some words are shown in bold, **like this**. You can find
out what they mean by looking in the Glossary.

Contents

My Diary

Friday, June 12—Seven days to go!

I'm so excited. There are just seven days before our new ballet opens. The ballet is called *The Nutcracker*, and I am dancing the **role** of the Sugar Plum Fairy.

We have been **rehearsing** in the studio for weeks. The final week is always very busy.

Practice at the Barre

Saturday, June 13—Six days to go!

I practiced this morning, as I do every single day. I **warmed up** at the **barre**. If I don't warm up carefully, I could injure myself. That would be a disaster!

Warming-up exercises help to warm up my muscles.

When I am **en pointe**, I balance on the tips of my toes in special shoes.

Then I practiced my pointe work. I practiced for longer than usual today. I want to be at my very best for the performance.

7

Center Work

When I finished my **barre** exercises, I moved into the center of the floor. Here I practiced balancing, turning, jumping, and moving my whole body.

I finished with **cooling-down** exercises. These are as important as **warming up**. I love dancing, even when I am only practicing.

The Theater

Sunday, June 14—Five days to go!

Today, we went to look around the theater where we will be performing. I looked at the empty seats and imagined what it would be like when they were full of people.

10

A dancer gets ready in the dressing room.

I did a few **pirouettes** on the stage before we went backstage. The dressing rooms have just been redecorated. They look amazing!

Talking to Students

Today, I talked to a class of ballet students about how ballet dancers look onstage. We wear special stage makeup. Our hair must be neat and pulled back off our faces.

Ballerinas often put on their own makeup.

Ballet dancers have to take care of themselves when they are not dancing. In addition to exercising, I always make sure I eat plenty of healthy food.

Hard Work

Tuesday, June 16—Three days to go!

A young girl asked me for my autograph as I left the studio. She asked me how I became a dancer. I told her I started ballet lessons when I was six years old.

I applied to join a ballet school when I was 12. I was nervous at the **audition**, but then I was very happy when I was accepted.

Joining a Ballet Company

When I left ballet school, I joined a big ballet company as a member of the **corps de ballet**. It was so exciting!

Carlos Acosta

Then I joined a smaller ballet company, where I now dance **solo** parts. My ambition is to get bigger **roles**. I would love to dance with Carlos Acosta. He is my favorite male dancer!

17

Dress Rehearsal

Wednesday, June 17—Two days to go!

We moved into the theater today. We practiced on the stage this morning. This evening we had a full **dress rehearsal** with the orchestra.

We wore our costumes and danced the whole ballet as though it were a real performance. There was even an audience, including some of my friends and family.

Final Fitting

Thursday, June 18—One day to go!

My costume felt a bit uncomfortable last night, so today I went to see the costume fitters. They were very busy today. There were **tutus** everywhere!

Then I tried on two new pairs of shoes that I bought for opening night tomorrow. They fit well, which was a relief.

Last-Minute Changes

The **choreographer** made some changes, too. He is the person who directs every step and move in the dance. He thought some of the movements needed more space on the stage.

George Balanchine

This meant we all had to change our positions. Sometimes I think he sees himself as George Balanchine—the most famous choreographer ever!

The Curtain Rises

Friday, June 19—Opening night!

Today, I was very excited and nervous, but doing my usual practice exercises helped to calm me down. Waiting for the performance to begin seemed to last forever.

At last, the music started, the curtain went up, and the ballet began. I watched from the **wings** and waited. When the music for my dance began, I entered the stage.

Cheering and Clapping

The music took me over and I danced as beautifully as I could. I wanted the audience to feel what the Sugar Plum Fairy felt.

At the end of the ballet, we all lined up onstage to take our final bows. People continued clapping and cheering. The main dancers were given bouquets of flowers. It was so thrilling!

Writing a Diary

You can write a diary, too! Your diary can describe your life—what you saw, what you felt, and the events that happened. You could even write an imaginary diary for one of your pets!

Writing a diary is a great way to help us remember the things that happened in our lives. You could pretend that your diary is a secret diary and begin with "Dear Diary"!

Here are some tips for writing a diary:

- Start each entry with the day and the date. You don't have to include an entry for every day.

- The entries should be in **chronological** order, which means that they follow the order in which events happened.

- Use the past tense when you are writing about something that has already happened.

- Remember that a diary is the writer's story, so use "I" and "my."

Glossary

audition test that includes performing. Dancers, actors, and other performers audition for parts or to be accepted into special schools.

barre long rail, often in front of a mirror, that ballet dancers hold onto while they practice

choreographer person who decides upon all the steps in a dance

chronological in order of time

cooling-down (exercises) exercises that allow your body to gently relax

corps de ballet group of dancers who dance together

dress rehearsal practice performance of a whole ballet, from start to finish. In a dress rehearsal, the dancers wear their costumes.

en pointe when a ballerina balances and dances on the tips of her toes, wearing special shoes

pirouette twirl or spin

rehearse practice performing something

role part (or character) in a ballet, play, movie, or other performance

solo performance done by one dancer on his or her own

tutu short, stiff skirt worn by a ballerina

warm up (exercises) exercises that gently move the parts of your body you are about to use

wings places at the sides of the stage that the audience cannot see

Find Out More

Books

Clay, Kathryn. *Ballet Dancing* (Pebble Plus). Mankato, Minn.: Capstone, 2010.

Graves, Karen M. *Ballet Dance* (Snap Books). Mankato, Minn.: Capstone, 2008.

Regan, Lisa. *Ballet Dancer* (Stage School). New York: Windmill, 2013.

Royston, Angela. *Ballet* (Love to Dance). Chicago: Raintree, 2013.

Internet sites

Facthound offers a safe, fun way to find Internet sites related to this book. All of the sites on Facthound have been researched by our staff.

Here's all you do:
Visit www.facthound.com
Type in this code: 9781432975791

Index